EARTH FIGURED OU

T0276813

Plant
Structures

Nancy Dickmann

Cavendish
Square

New York

Published in 2016 by Cavendish Square Publishing, LLC
243 5th Avenue, Suite 136, New York, NY 10016

Website: cavendishsq.com

This publication represents the opinions and views of the author based on his or her personal
experience, knowledge, and research. The information in this book serves as a general guide only.
The author and publisher have used their best efforts in preparing this book and disclaim liability
rising directly or indirectly from the use and application of this book.

CPSIA Compliance Information: Batch #CW16CSQ

All websites were available and accurate when this book was sent to press.

Cataloging-in-Publication Data

Dickmann, Nancy.
Plant structures / by Nancy Dickmann.
p. cm. — (Earth figured out)
Includes index.
ISBN 978-1-5026-0876-5 (hardcover) ISBN 978-1-5026-0874-1 (paperback)
ISBN 978-1-5026-0877-2 (ebook)
1. Plants — Juvenile literature. 2. Plant anatomy — Juvenile literature. I. Dickmann, Nancy. II. Title.
QK49.D53 2016
580—d23

Produced for Cavendish Square by Calcium
Editors: Sarah Eason and Harriet McGregor
Designer: Paul Myerscough

Picture credits: amenic181/Shutterstock.com, cover; Insides: Shutterstock: 5 Second Studio 21,
Aaltair 20–21, Adistock 16, Jeff Baumgart 26–27, Dariush M 16–17, Angel DiBilio 29, Fotokostic
1, 24–25, Zack Frank 9, Christopher Gardiner 25, Jubal Harshaw 26, Maxim Ibragimov 6–7,
Kan_khampanya 5, Dudarev Mikhail 12–13, Boris Mrdja 12, Quick Shot 4–5, Pres Panayotov
18–19, Siambizkit 8–9, Snapgalleria 14–15, Wang Song 28–29, Craig Sterken 22–23b, Praiwun
Thungsarn 10, Bogdan Wankowicz 7, Welcomia 11, Pan Xunbin 15, Yogo 19; Wikimedia
Commons: 22–23t.

Printed in the United States of America

Contents

A World of Plants

From space, our home planet looks like a blue and green ball. The blue is the oceans, but the green color is caused by the plants that cover huge areas of land. There are even plants living in the oceans!

The number of different plants on Earth is truly amazing. From tiny one-celled algae to the tallest trees, plants can live in all sorts of different habitats. Some are **adapted** to live in deserts, where there is very little water. Others are able to live in cold, windy tundra regions.

Although plants can be very different, most of them have similar structures. Many well-known plants make flowers and seeds. They have stems, roots, and leaves, and they are able to transport water and **nutrients** throughout their structures. However, there are also many other types of plants, such as mosses. They have different structures and life cycles.

EARTH FIGURED OUT

The smallest known flowering plant is a type of duckweed called watermeal. These tiny plants are each about the size of a candy sprinkle. In contrast, the world's tallest tree is about as high as a forty story building!

These lupines are a typical example of a flowering plant. They have roots, a stem, and leaves, and they produce flowers and seeds in order to **reproduce**.

A plant can live on its own, but usually plants are found in groups of thousands or millions of separate **organisms**, like this forest.

Seeds and Shoots

These prickly burrs contain the plant's seeds. They may get stuck to an animal's fur before falling off and growing into a new plant.

Many plants start life as a seed. The seed is produced by a mature plant, and it will sprout into a new plant of the same type. Most seeds have a tough outer covering that protects them, as well a store of food for the young plant to use. Most importantly, they have something called an **embryo**, which will grow into a new plant.

A seed can stay **dormant** for a long time before it **germinates**, or starts to grow. Germination only happens when the conditions are right. A seed needs water, oxygen, and warmth to germinate.

When a seed **absorbs** water, the parts inside it start to swell. This causes the outer covering to split. The first root starts growing downward, into the soil. A shoot grows upward, and the first one or two leaves unfold. The young plant produces more roots and more leaves, and it grows quickly.

For many plants, the shape of the seed depends on how it will travel to the place where it takes root. For example, a maple tree's seeds are blown by the wind, and they are shaped like wings. Some types of seeds can float. Others have tiny hooks that cling to an animal's fur.

The roots' job is to take in water and other nutrients that the plant needs. The leaves absorb sunlight and make food for the plant.

Roots

Roots are the first part of a plant to sprout from the seed, and they are very important. Without roots, a plant could not take in moisture and nutrients from the ground. Roots also anchor, or hold, a plant in the ground and keep it from blowing or washing away.

Different plants have different types of roots. In some plants, including trees, the first root grows straight down. Smaller roots soon grow out sideways from it. The root system looks like an upside-down version of a tree trunk, with smaller branches coming out from it. Other types of plants, such as grasses, have a thick clump of roots that are all about the same size. These plants do not have a main root.

In some plants, roots are able to store food for the plant, and they often become big and swollen. We eat many of these roots, including carrots, radishes, parsnips, and turnips.

EARTH FIGURED OUT

Some plants do not send roots down into the ground. Instead, they are able to get the water and minerals they need from the air, and from **debris** that collects on the plants that support them. These types of plants are called epiphytes or "air plants."

You can often see epiphytes, such as this Spanish moss, on tree branches. The tree provides physical support for the epiphyte.

Sometimes part of a tree's root system will be visible above the ground.

ROOTS AND SHOOTS—FIGURED OUT!

A single watermeal plant weighs about

1/190,000

of an ounce (0.00015 grams). This is roughly equal to two grains of salt! It would take 5,000 of the plants just to fill a thimble.

The seeds of some plants are so small that they are more like dust than seeds. Some types of orchids have seeds that weigh

1/35,000,000

of an ounce (0.00000079 g). They are 1/300 of an inch (0.0083 centimeters) long— far too small to see without a microscope.

Roots can be huge. The longest carrot ever grown was 19 feet 1.96 inches (5.84 meters) long. The heaviest carrot on record weighed

20

pounds (9 kilograms). However, that's a lightweight compared to the world's heaviest beet, at 51 pounds 9.4 ounces (23.4 kg), and the world's heaviest rutabaga, at 85 pounds 8 ounces (38.8 kg).

In some plants, pressure builds up inside the seedpod until it explodes, sending seeds in all directions. The sandbox tree can shoot seeds more than

150 feet (46 m).

There is a grove of aspen trees in Utah that share the same massive root system, making it a single organism. The grove covers

106 acres

(43 hectares), with more than 40,000 separate trunks. Scientists think that the aspens weigh 1.3 million pounds (5.9 million kg) in total.

LET'S FIGURE OUT ...

Leaves

Leaves are one of a plant's most important parts. They grow out from the stem and branches, and their main job is making food for the plant to use. They also allow the plant to take in and release gases, such as water vapor.

Leaves come in many shapes and sizes, but most have a broad, flat part called a blade. A stalk (also called a petiole) attaches the blade to the plant's stem. Some leaves are simple, with only one blade. Others are more complicated, with several blades attached to a single stalk. Some leaves are smooth and waxy, and others are hairy. Some leaves are even prickly!

Most leaves are green, and they get their color from a substance called **chlorophyll**. In some trees, the leaves lose their chlorophyll in the fall. Eventually, they turn brown and dry, and fall off. New leaves grow in the spring. However, some types of trees keep their leaves all year long.

The needles on a pine tree let heavy snow slide off the tree so that it does not become weighed down.

12

When a leaf loses its chlorophyll, its red, orange, and yellow pigments become visible. This creates beautiful fall colors.

EARTH FIGURED OUT

Not all leaves are broad and flat. The long, thin needles on pine trees are a special type of leaf. They are adapted to survive in harsher, colder conditions than broad leaves, and they do not fall off in the winter.

Photosynthesis

Leaves help a plant make its own food, in a process called **photosynthesis**. In photosynthesis, a plant uses the **energy** in sunlight to turn water and **carbon dioxide** into chemicals called **carbohydrates**. These carbohydrates store energy in a form that a plant's **cells** can use to grow.

Most leaves are broad and flat, which lets them take in as much sunlight as possible. They also have a lot of tiny holes, called **stomata**, on their undersides. Gases can pass through these holes, and this is how the plant takes in carbon dioxide from the air. The plant's roots take in water, and the chlorophyll in the leaves helps to absorb sunlight.

Once all the ingredients are in place, a **chemical reaction** takes place inside a plant's leaves. Each cell contains structures called **chloroplasts**, which are where the plant's chlorophyll is found. The chemical reaction takes place in the chloroplasts.

This diagram shows how photosynthesis works.

EARTH FIGURED OUT

All life on Earth depends on photosynthesis. Without it, plants could not survive, and, with no plants to eat, animals could not survive either.

In photosynthesis, plants also take carbon dioxide from the air and replace it with oxygen. All animals need oxygen to breathe.

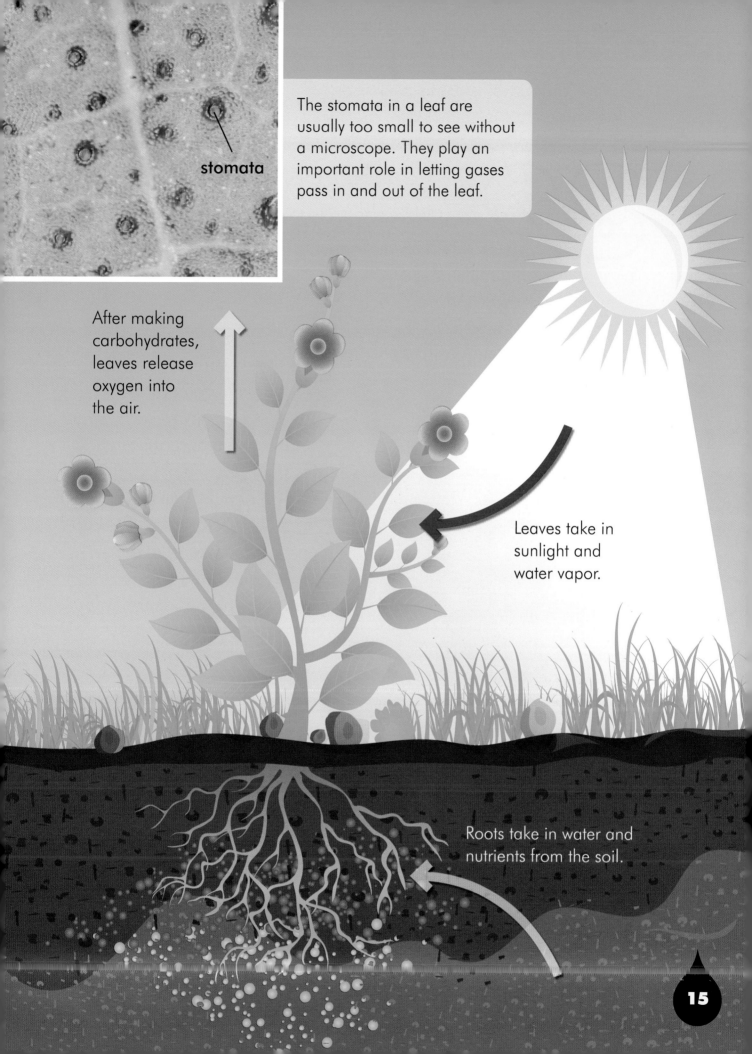

stomata

The stomata in a leaf are usually too small to see without a microscope. They play an important role in letting gases pass in and out of the leaf.

After making carbohydrates, leaves release oxygen into the air.

Leaves take in sunlight and water vapor.

Roots take in water and nutrients from the soil.

LEAVES—FIGURED OUT!

Leaves come in all shapes and sizes, but the leaves of the raffia palm are true record-breakers. They can reach a massive

82 feet (25 m) long.

The leaves of a Californian wildflower called pygmy weed are much smaller: about 0.047 inches (0.12 cm) long.

Too much carbon dioxide in the atmosphere contributes to climate change. An average-sized mature tree can absorb

48 pounds (22 kg)

of carbon dioxide in a year. At the same time, it releases enough oxygen into the atmosphere for two people to breathe.

Most clover plants have three or four leaves. However, the record for the most leaves on a clover is

56 leaves!

A large apple tree may have between 50,000 and

100,000

leaves. However, other types of trees have many more. An old oak tree can have 700,000 and a mature American elm might have 5 million!

The stomata on a leaf are far too small to see without a powerful microscope. The leaf of an apple tree has around

300

stomata in an area of just 0.0015 square inches (1 square millimeters)!

Flowers

Beautiful flowers come in an amazing range of colors and shapes, and they all have an important role. Their job is to produce seeds. Seeds allow the plant to reproduce and pass on its **traits** to the next generation.

Most flowers have both male and female parts. The male parts make **pollen**. The female parts make seeds, but to do this they need pollen from another flower. Insects, birds, and other animals sometimes help to take pollen from one flower to another. When they land on a flower, pollen rubs off onto their bodies. When they fly to another flower, some of the pollen rubs off onto the flower's female parts.

Plants need to make themselves attractive to pollinators. They can do this by providing food, such as **nectar**. They might also have bright colors and a strong scent to make themselves stand out. Some flowers are shaped in a way that makes it easier for certain types of insects to land on them.

EARTH FIGURED OUT

Not all plants have flowers. Some, such as pine trees, make seeds without flowers. Their seeds are kept safe in woody cones. Other plants, such as ferns and mosses, produce spores instead of seeds. You may be able to see tiny, round spores on the underside of a fern's leaf.

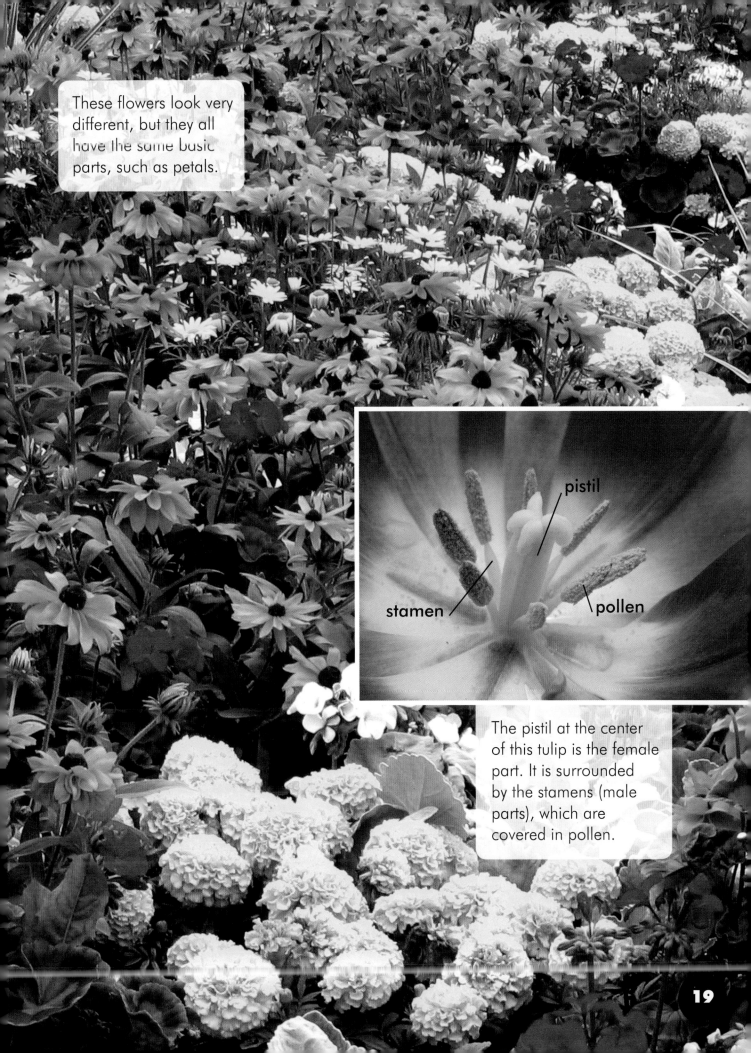

These flowers look very different, but they all have the same basic parts, such as petals.

pistil

stamen

pollen

The pistil at the center of this tulip is the female part. It is surrounded by the stamens (male parts), which are covered in pollen.

LET'S FIGURE OUT ...
Fruits

The female parts of a flower are at the center. When the flower is pollinated, these parts start to grow into a fruit. Some parts become seeds, and the parts surrounding them become the rest of the fruit. The fruit protects the seeds inside. It also helps to **disperse** the seeds so that they can sprout into new plants.

Fruits and seeds are incredibly important to humans because we eat them for energy. Nuts, peas, and beans are all seeds. The list of fruits we eat is very long: apples, cucumbers, oranges, bananas, tomatoes, lemons, and avocados are just a few. In most of these fruits you can see the seeds they contain when you cut into them.

Many fruits help to disperse seeds. For example, the coconut that you see at the store is a seed that was once inside a lightweight fruit. The fruit can float, and this allows coconut seeds to travel long distances across the oceans before sprouting.

An orange tree grows from a single seed, but it can produce hundreds of oranges every year. Each one will contain several seeds.

EARTH FIGURED OUT

Many birds and other animals eat fruits. When they do, they also eat the seeds inside the fruit. Their bodies digest the flesh of the fruit, but the seeds inside often come out in their waste. This can happen a long way from where they found the fruit. These seeds may then grow into new plants.

20

Most fruits have the seeds on the inside, though they can be arranged in different ways. This kiwi fruit has the seeds on the inside.

PLANT REPRODUCTION—FIGURED OUT!

The largest single flower in the world belongs to the *Rafflesia* plant. It can be **3** feet (1 m) across and weigh up to 15 pounds 6.8 kg). The *Titan arum*'s flower is even bigger, but it is actually a cluster of many tiny flowers. It can grow up to 12 feet (3.6 m) tall and weigh 170 pounds (77 kg).

Some fruits are truly enormous! The world's largest bean pods can be up to **5** feet (1.5 m) long. The largest pumpkin ever grown weighed 2,323 pounds (1,054 kg).

Grains of pollen are extremely tiny; most are only 0.0004 to 0.004 inches (10 to 100 microns) in diameter. A human hair is around 0.002 inches (50 microns) wide. Some pollen grains are much narrower than a hair!

Many plants produce flowers every year, but some blooms are much rarer. The kurinji is a bluish-purple flower found in India. It only blooms once every 12 years. The talipot palm grows for up to 80 years before it blooms for the first time. Once the fruit appears, the plant dies.

Fruits such as peaches and avocados contain only 1 seed. Others have many more: most apples have between 2 and 15 seeds, and kiwis, watermelons, and pomegranates have several hundred.

Stems

A stem holds most plants upright. The tiny shoot that first sprouts from a seed will eventually grow and thicken into a sturdy stem. The stem holds the plant's leaves and flowers up, and it can keep the leaves in a position that receives the most sunlight. Branches and leaves grow out from the stem.

Some plants have flexible green stems, and others have hard, woody stems. Plants with soft stems usually die each year. For example, a tomato plant will die when the growing season finishes. In the spring, you need to plant one of its seeds to get a new tomato plant. An apple tree, on the other hand, will lose its leaves in the fall, but the woody trunk remains alive. It will sprout new leaves and flowers in the spring.

EARTH FIGURED OUT

Some plants' stems do several different jobs. For example, photosynthesis takes place in the stem of a cactus. The stem is also important for storing water. During the rare times when there is rain in a desert, the stem can swell to hold as much water as possible. When the plant uses this water during dry periods, the stem contracts, or shrinks.

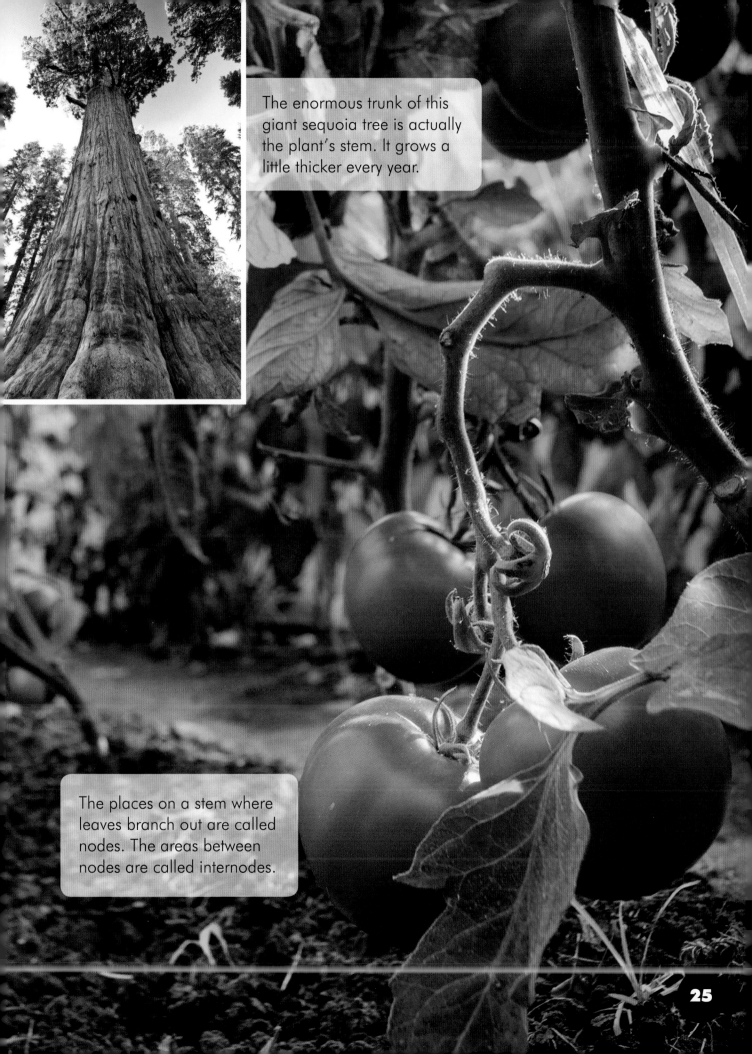

The enormous trunk of this giant sequoia tree is actually the plant's stem. It grows a little thicker every year.

The places on a stem where leaves branch out are called nodes. The areas between nodes are called internodes.

Transportation

Aside from holding a plant up, the stems of many plants have another job. They make it possible for water and nutrients to travel through the plant. They can do this because of two special **tissues** they contain: **xylem** (said ZIE-lem) and **phloem** (FLOW-em). These parts are a little like the blood vessels that carry blood around your body.

A plant's roots take in water and **dissolved** nutrients from the soil. These substances travel up the xylem to reach the plant's branches and leaves, like water being sucked up through a straw. The water eventually **evaporates** from the leaves. Meanwhile, the leaves use photosynthesis to produce the plant's food, in the form of sugars. These sugars travel through the phloem to reach the parts of the plant where they are needed—either for growing new tissues or to be stored to use later.

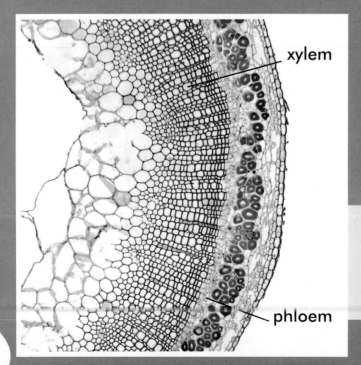

xylem

phloem

The sap from a maple tree is only about 2 percent sugar. It takes 30 to 40 gallons (113 to 151 Liters) of sap to make just 1 gallon (4 L) of maple syrup.

This magnified cross-section of a flax stem shows the xylem and phloem.

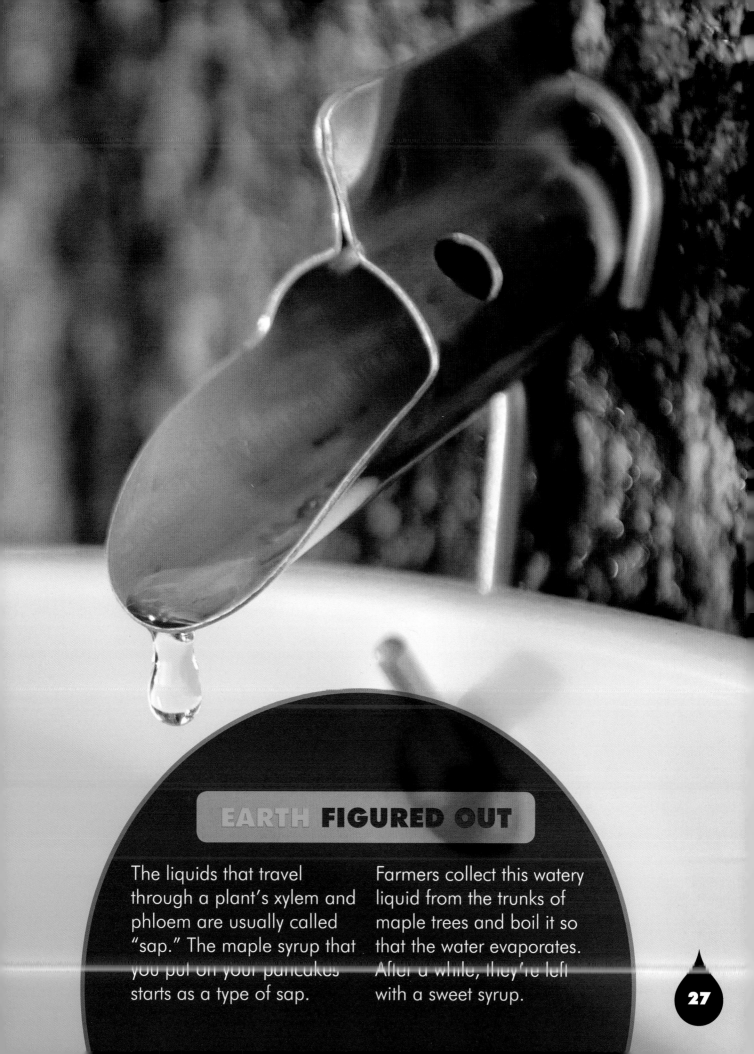

EARTH FIGURED OUT

The liquids that travel through a plant's xylem and phloem are usually called "sap." The maple syrup that you put on your pancakes starts as a type of sap.

Farmers collect this watery liquid from the trunks of maple trees and boil it so that the water evaporates. After a while, they're left with a sweet syrup.

Working Together

Each part of a plant has a job to do. The roots take in moisture and nutrients from the soil, and the xylem in the plant's stem carries them to the other parts of the plant. The leaves make food for the plant, and the phloem transports the food. Flowers make seeds and fruit to help the plant reproduce. All the parts must work together. It's like the way that your heart, lungs, muscles, bones, and other body parts work together to keep you alive.

However, there are some types of plants that don't have all of these structures. Many plants don't make seeds at all. Some plants, such as pine trees, don't have flowers but still make seeds. Mosses are an example of a plant without a true stem, and the tiny algae that float in the oceans don't have leaves or roots. These plants all have different ways to survive in their habitats.

Each of these sunflowers has different parts working together to help it grow tall and make seeds.

EARTH FIGURED OUT

Sometimes plants must work together with animals to survive. For example, a bee helps to pollinate a plant and gets nectar to eat in return.

The bullhorn acacia plant provides food and shelter for a type of ant, which protect the plant from animals that might want to eat it.

Both the ants and the bullhorn acacia plant benefit from living together. This type of relationship is called mutualism.

Glossary

absorbs Takes in.

adapted Having changed over time in a way that helps the organism to survive and reproduce in its habitat.

carbohydrates Substances made of carbon, hydrogen, and oxygen, which can be used to produce and store energy.

carbon dioxide A gas breathed out by animals, which plants need in order to make food.

cells The smallest units of a living thing. Plants and animals are made up of cells.

chemical reaction The process in which one or more substances change into new substances.

chlorophyll The green matter in the leaves and stems of plants that helps them produce food from sunlight.

chloroplasts The structures in a plant's cells that contain chlorophyll.

debris Waste.

disperse To send out.

dissolved When a substance mixed with a liquid becomes part of the liquid.

dormant Not active. A seed can stay dormant for many years before germinating.

embryo A new plant that is just starting to develop. Plant embryos are found inside seeds.

energy The ability to do work.

evaporates When a liquid turns into a gas and rises into the air.

germinates When a growing plant from a seed.

nectar A sweet substance made by plants.

nutrients Substances that a living thing needs in order to grow and stay healthy.

organisms Living things, such as plants or animals.

phloem The soft tissue in some plants that carries food from the leaves to the rest of the plant.

photosynthesis The process in which a plant uses sunlight to change water and carbon dioxide into food for itself.

pollen The sticky powder made by flowers that helps them form seeds.

reproduce To have offspring.

stomata Tiny holes on the underside of a plant's leaf that allow water and gases to move in and out.

tissues Groups of cells in an animal's or a plant's body that are similar to each other and do similar things.

traits Characteristics that make a living thing different from others of the same type, for example, height or leaf shape.

xylem The soft tissue in some plants that carries water and nutrients from the roots to the rest of the plant.

Further Reading

Books

Burnie, David. *Eyewitness Plant.* DK Eyewitness Books. New York: DK Children, 2011.

Higgins, Nadia. *Experiment with Parts of a Plant.* Lightning Bolt Books. Minneapolis, MN: Lerner Publishing Group, 2015.

Levine, Shar. *Plants: Flowering Plants, Ferns, Mosses, and Other Plants.* Class of Their Own. New York: Crabtree Publishing Company, 2010.

Lynette, Rachel. *Plants.* The Science Behind. Chicago: Raintree, 2012.

Slingerland, Janet. *The Secret Lives of Plants!* Adventures in Science. Mankato, MN: Capstone Press, 2014.

Websites

This website from the US Department of Agriculture has lots of great ideas for science projects about plants:
www.ars.usda.gov/is/kids/AgSciProjects/ideas.htm

Find more details about plant parts and processes here:
www.biology4kids.com/files/plants_main.html

On this interactive site, you can identify different species of wildflowers that you may have seen growing:
www.discoverlife.org/mp/20q?guide=Wildflowers

This YouTube channel has videos about a range of amazing plants, hosted by a botany professor:
www.youtube.com/user/PlantsAreCoolToo

Index